Did You Invent the Phone Alone, Alexander Graham Bell?

Melvin and Gilda Berger
illustrated by Brandon Dorman

SCHOLASTIC NONFICTION
an imprint of
SCHOLASTIC

Contents

How did Alexander Graham Bell change the world?

Alexander Graham Bell invented the telephone in 1876. He was twenty-nine years old. For the first time, people could speak to each other over long distances. Families and friends could keep in touch and share information. Business and industry could expand all around the world.

Alexander Graham Bell did not work alone on the invention of the telephone. He hired Thomas Watson to help him. Watson knew a great deal about electricity. Together they built the first telephone. Two other Americans, Elisha Gray and Antonio Meucci, also get credit for inventing telephones at about the same time.

Alexander Graham Bell

When was Bell born?

Alexander Bell was born in Edinburgh, Scotland, on March 3, 1847. His parents were Alexander Melville and Eliza Grace Bell. They named him Alexander but called him Aleck. Aleck's parents had three sons and

no daughters. Aleck was the middle child, born between Melville (nicknamed Melly) in 1845 and Edward (often called Ted) in 1848.

Alexander Bell at age 11, about the time he added the middle name of Graham.

The Bell family (from left to right): Melville James (Aleck's older brother), Alexander Melville (father), Edward (younger brother), Eliza (mother), and Alexander Graham Bell.

When Aleck was eleven, a family friend, Alexander Graham, came to visit. Aleck liked him so much that he decided to use the name Graham as his middle name. From then on, he was known as Alexander Graham Bell.

Who influenced Aleck the most?

Aleck's father and grandfather had the greatest influence on him. They were both interested in communication — especially speech and hearing. Aleck's grandfather taught others to overcome speech problems and speak more clearly. He inspired his son, Aleck's father, to follow in his footsteps.

Three generations of the Bell family (from left to right): grandfather (Alexander Bell), Alexander Graham Bell, and father (Alexander Melville Bell).

Aleck's father worked out a method to improve the speech of deaf people and others with speech problems. He called it Visible Speech. The method used symbols to show

ways of forming the mouth, tongue, and lips to make different sounds and words. Alexander Melville's interest in hearing grew when he met and married Eliza Grace Symonds. She had been nearly deaf since childhood.

Visible Speech symbols for various numbers, objects, and short phrases.

Was Aleck smart?

Aleck was very smart. But he wasn't a very good student. He was, however, very curious about many things — especially sound. One of his earliest memories was sitting in a wheatfield and listening for the sound of wheat growing!

Aleck had a loud, booming voice. Yet his mother could not hear him, even through a hearing tube that she held to her ear. One day, Aleck had a great idea. He held his mouth close to his mother's forehead and talked loudly. The bones of her head carried the sound into her ear, and she heard what he said. From this experience, Aleck learned more about how sound travels and how sounds reach the ear.

Aleck's way of speaking to his mother worked better than using her hearing tube to make sounds louder.

Aleck and his brothers probably saw this elaborate "speaking machine," made by Joseph Faber around 1840. Faber operated his Euphonia with foot pedals and a keyboard. The wooden carving of the turbaned lady was just for show. The Bells' machine resembled the Euphonia, but was much simpler.

What were Aleck's first experiments with sound?

At age fourteen, Aleck and his brothers saw a "speaking machine" in London. It was able to make a number of human sounds and even "speak" some simple words. Back home, the boys' father suggested that they build their own speaking machine. The machine they built made sounds like a crying baby. In fact, their neighbors thought that Mrs. Bell had had another child!

Next, Aleck tried an experiment on his own. He massaged his dog's throat so that it made growls that sounded like words. The dog seemed to say, "How are you, Grandma?"

Did Aleck do more work with speech?

In October 1862, Aleck's parents sent him to London to spend a year studying speech with his grandfather. While there, he also

learned more about sound and electricity. He began teaching at a school for hearing-disabled children. He also studied at London University for a while.

At age 15, the time of this photo, Aleck had already invented a tool to remove husks from wheat.

Then Aleck returned to Scotland. He traveled with his father and brothers throughout the country putting on a show that used Visible Speech. The boys would leave the room, and Aleck's father would ask people in the audience to call out different words. For each word, he drew the symbols. When the boys came back in, they looked at the symbols and tried to say the words. The boys got the words right almost every time!

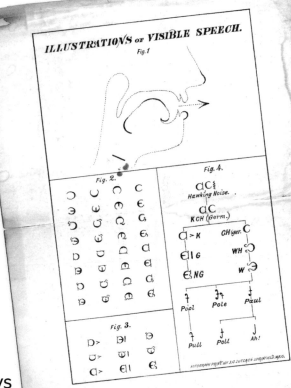

This Visible Speech chart shows some of the symbols that Aleck's grandfather created to teach the deaf. Each symbol showed exactly how to shape the tongue and lips to make a particular sound.

The Bells' house in Canada. Aleck's mother is
seated on the left and his father is in the buggy.

What tragedy struck the Bell family?

During the following years, Aleck was very busy studying and teaching speech. At that time, both of his brothers died of tuberculosis, a lung disease. When Aleck seemed to be getting sick, too, his parents decided to move to Canada. They felt that Canada's fresh, clean air would protect Aleck against the sickness. In the summer of 1870, the family moved to Brantford, Ontario, in Canada.

The Bells bought a large farmhouse. Aleck called it his "dreaming place." Here he did more experiments with sound. In one, he sang different notes with his mouth close to the piano strings and heard the piano "sing" back the same notes.

When did Bell come to the United States?

In March 1871, Bell took a job in Boston teaching deaf children. He used Visible Speech and his own methods to teach the students, as well as other teachers.

He scored a big success with a student named Georgie Sanders, who was born deaf. Bell started working with five-year-old Georgie in 1872. Aleck taught the boy to read. He also wrote out the alphabet on a glove so Georgie could point to the letters and "talk" in that way.

In October 1873, Bell began teaching

Flyer offering speech
instruction by Bell
and his father.

at Boston University. He used a device called a phonoautograph. Students who were deaf, hard of hearing, or wanted to improve their speech spoke into the instrument and saw the patterns made by the sounds. From this, they learned how to make better sounds.

Bell (top right) poses with teachers and students at the Boston School for the Deaf in 1871.

Try it out!
Experiment #1: What is sound?

Sound is what you hear when something shakes back and forth very fast, or vibrates. Lightly hold your hand on the front of your throat. Now say the word "telephone." Do you feel the shaking inside your throat? It is your vocal cords vibrating. These vibrations make sound waves that spread out through the air.

Some of these sound waves reach your ear. They make the bones in your ear vibrate. The vibrations send a message to your brain.

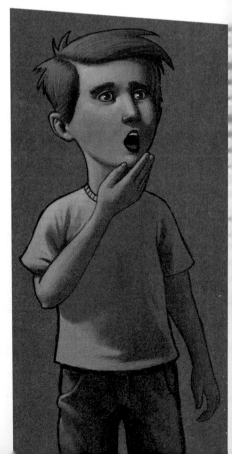

Try it out!

Experiment #2: See the sound waves of your voice

You'll need a can opener, a large, clean, empty metal can, a rubber balloon, a rubber band, scissors, glue, and a small square of shiny, smooth, new aluminum foil.

1. Remove the bottom of the can *very carefully*.

2. Cut off the neck of the balloon. Stretch the balloon very tightly over one end of the can. Fix it in place with the rubber band.

3. Glue the aluminum foil, *shiny side out*, onto the middle of the stretched balloon.

4. Stand so sunlight from a window shines on the foil. Hold the can so that the reflection makes a bright spot on a wall.

5. Sing loudly into the open end of the can and watch the reflections shake.

What happened to Bell when he was in Boston?

While teaching at Boston University, Bell studied electricity on his own. He hoped to find a way to improve the telegraph, which sends dot-and-dash messages, but not speech, through electrical wires. Bell wanted to send several telegraph messages over the same wire at the same time. This would let several people use one wire at the same time instead of one person at a time. Thomas Alva Edison, the inventor of the electric lightbulb, also worked on sending several telegraph messages through one wire.

In Boston, Bell met two people who were to become very important in his life. One was Mabel Hubbard, who had lost her hearing when she was four. She would later become his wife.

He also met Thomas Watson, who was working in a shop that made electrical instruments. Bell hired Watson to become his assistant. Watson's knowledge of electricity played an important part in Bell's success.

Above: Mabel Hubbard, Bell's future wife; her father helped support Bell's early work.
Right: Thomas Watson, Bell's partner in his lab, holds a model of the first telephone.

What accident led Bell to the idea of a telephone?

On June 2, 1875, Bell and Watson were communicating by telegraph in separate rooms. A thin piece of metal got stuck in Watson's equipment. As he pulled it out, Bell heard a *ping*. He realized the sound came through the wire from Watson's room. Quickly Bell ran in, shouting, "Watson, what did you do then? Don't change anything."

The men continued their experiments. They could send sounds, but not words, through the wire. Bell feared that someone else might invent the telephone first. So, in February 1876, he applied for a telephone patent, even though the invention wasn't ready. A patent is issued by the U.S. government; it says that only the inventor can make or sell the invention.

Bell is surprised to hear a *ping* — the first sound ever sent by electricity!

What happened next?

Bell received his telephone patent on March 7, 1876. He and Watson had worked to improve the machine all fall and winter. But they still had not succeeded. People could hear a voice on the telephone but could not understand what was being said.

But Bell was lucky. He already had the patent for the telephone. Just a few hours after he put in his application, Elisha Gray asked for a telephone patent. The few hours made all the difference. Bell got the patent; Gray did not.

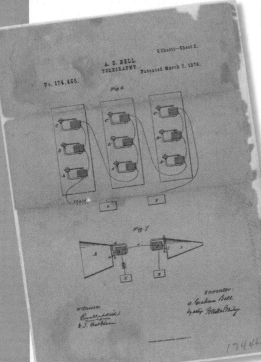

Right: Birthplace of the telephone Bell's lab was on the top floor of this building on Court Street in Boston, Massachusetts

Above: A page of Bell's patent application.

Who made the first telephone call?

Bell and Watson kept on working and improving the telephone. On March 10, 1876, Bell was trying to send a voice message to Watson, who was in another room with a receiver. Bell wanted to see if it would help

The transmitter of the first words sent by telephone.

to keep part of the wire in battery acid. Accidentally, he spilled some acid on his pants. He shouted into the mouthpiece,

"Mr. Watson — come here — I want you!"

Watson raced into the room. He had heard Bell over the wires! The new telephone had carried Bell's voice and words. Alexander Graham Bell had made the first telephone call in history. Both men forgot the accident as Bell danced wildly around the room!

Bell's lab notebook from the breakthrough day, March 10, 1876.

When was the first long-distance telephone call?

In the summer of 1876, Bell went back to his home in Brantford, Canada. He set about trying to improve the telephone so that it would reach farther than room to room. In one early experiment, he sent a message over telegraph wires that were already in place. The wires connected his home in Brantford with the telegraph office in Mount Pleasant, a distance of about 5 miles (8 km).

The voice was not very clear or loud. But Bell could understand everything said by the people in Mount Pleasant. The first "long-distance" telephone call was a success! Still, Bell continued working to make the sound even better.

Alexander Graham Bell in 1876, at 29 years of age. During this important year, Bell received the patent for the telephone and spoke to Watson through a telephone for the first time.

31

What happens when you telephone a friend?

When you dial the number and say, "Hello," your vocal cords vibrate and send out sound waves. The waves pass through the air and into the telephone mouthpiece. The vibrations hit a thin metal disk. The sound waves make the disk vibrate. Electricity is always flowing through the disk. As the disk shakes back and forth, it sends out a pattern of big and small bursts of electricity.

If you're using a land phone, the bursts of electricity go through wires to a computer in the central telephone office for that area. If you're using a cell phone or cordless phone, the bursts go through the air as radio signals to the same computer. The computer then sends the bursts — through wires or as radio signals — to your friend's land phone, cell phone, or the base unit of a cordless phone.

Over the years, cell phones have become smaller, better, more reliable, and usable almost anywhere.

How does your friend hear you?

In a flash, the bursts of electricity reach your friend's telephone. They go into the earpiece. The earpiece also has a disk. The bursts of electricity make this disk vibrate. Back and forth the disk shakes. The shaking disk produces sound waves.

These sound waves are for the word "hello." The sound waves come out through the small holes of the earpiece. They strike your friend's ear and your friend hears you say, "Hello."

Today's cell phones can also serve as computers, cameras, clocks, and much, much more.

When did Bell get married?

Bell married his former student, Mabel Hubbard, on July 11, 1877. Mabel was born with normal hearing. At age four, though, she fell ill with a disease that left her deaf. She became very good at reading lips and was able to carry on conversations. But people found it hard to understand what she was saying. When Mabel was fifteen, her father brought her to Bell for speech lessons.

As the student and teacher came to know each other, they grew very close. The couple married and sailed to England, where they lived for one year. On their return, they moved to Washington, D.C.; the first of their four children was born there. Of the four, two girls survived, but two boys died as infants.

Mabel and Alexander Graham Bell with their two daughters, Elsie May (born 1878) on the left and Marian (born 1880) in the middle.

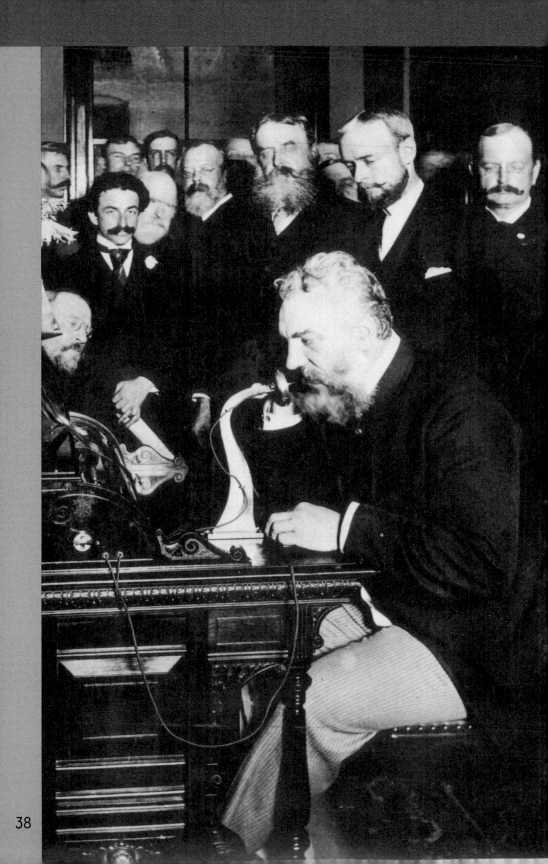

When did telephone service start in the United States?

On July 9, 1877, Bell, Watson, and a few others formed the Bell Telephone Company. For the first time, people could call one another on the telephone. Some said the telephone was "the most wonderful thing in America!"

CITY HALL, LAWRENCE, MASS.
Monday Evening, May 28

THE MIRACLE

WONDERFUL   TELEPHONE   DISCOVERY

TELEPHONE

OF THE AGE

Prof. A. Graham Bell, assisted by Mr. Frederic A. Gower, will give an exhibition of his wonderful and miraculous discovery The Telephone, before the people of Lawrence as above, when Boston and Lawrence will be connected via the Western Union Telegraph and vocal and instrumental music and conversation will be transmitted a distance of 27 miles and received by the audience in the City Hall.
Prof. Bell will give an explanatory lecture with this marvellous exhibition.

Cards of Admission, 35 cents
Reserved Seats, 50 cents

Sale of seats at Stratton's will open at 9 o'clock.

Facsimile of Flier Advertising Prof. Bell's Lecture at Lawrence, Mass., Monday Evening, May 28, 1877

A flyer advertising a public demonstration of the newly invented telephone.

The telephone also helped many businesses grow bigger and make more money. Workers and customers in all parts of the country could now speak to one another. They could buy and sell materials and products far more quickly than before.

Alexander Graham Bell sends a message across the long-distance line from New York to Chicago on the line's first day of operation.

Did Bell invent anything after the telephone?

Bell came up with other inventions, but none as important as the telephone. The photophone of 1880, for example, was able

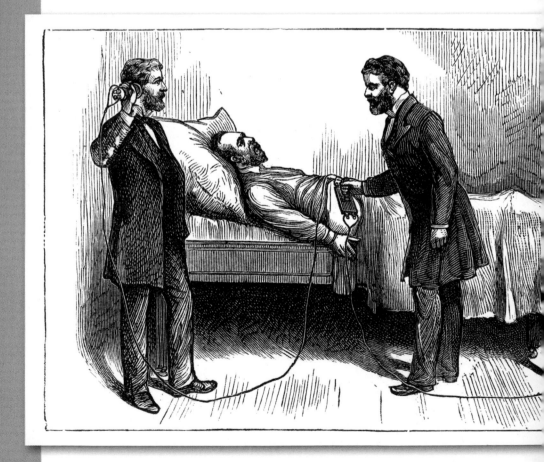

to send sound on a beam of light. Today scientists use this idea in fiber optics. Bell called it "the greatest invention I have ever made, greater than the telephone."

Another invention, which Bell called a telephonic probe, clicked loudly near

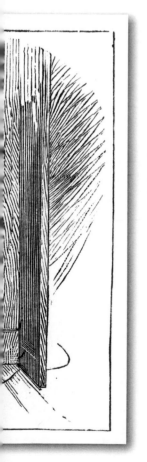

metal. It was widely used on patients who had been shot, to locate bullets. He also created a vacuum jacket to help people who had difficulty breathing, and an audiometer, to measure people's hearing. In addition, he worked on ways to make drinking water out of seawater, and to get liquid water from people's breaths.

Bell (right) is shown using his newly invented telephonic probe to try to locate the bullet that wounded, and later killed, President James Garfield.

How has the telephone been improved since Bell?

In 1965 Teri Pall invented a cordless phone. The cordless phone needs a land-phone base and can be used within about 2 miles (3.2 km) of the base. Some six years later, Martin Cooper built a battery-operated phone that was completely portable. Since then, many others have improved these ancestors of the cell phone.

Today, cell phones outnumber land phones and cordless phones. Telephone companies have divided the entire world into separate parts, or cells. The companies automatically pass signals from one cell to another. This lets you speak cell phone to cell phone almost anywhere in your country. With a special card in your cell phone you can make calls to about 200 other countries.

Dishes like these, on tall towers or on top of buildings, send and receive radio signals from cell phones.

How long did Alexander Graham Bell live?

Bell died on August 2, 1922, at age 75. He was buried at his home in Nova Scotia, Canada. Bell became a U.S. citizen in 1882, but he spent most of his later years in Nova Scotia working in his home laboratory. The lab never had a telephone. Bell was afraid it would interrupt his work!

When Bell died, all the telephones in the United States stopped ringing for one minute to honor his memory. Bell once offered these wise words about life and inventing: "Leave the beaten track occasionally and dive into the woods. Every time you do so you will be certain to find something you have never seen before."

Alexander Graham Bell writing at his desk a few weeks before he died at his summer home in Beinn Bhreagh, Nova Scotia.

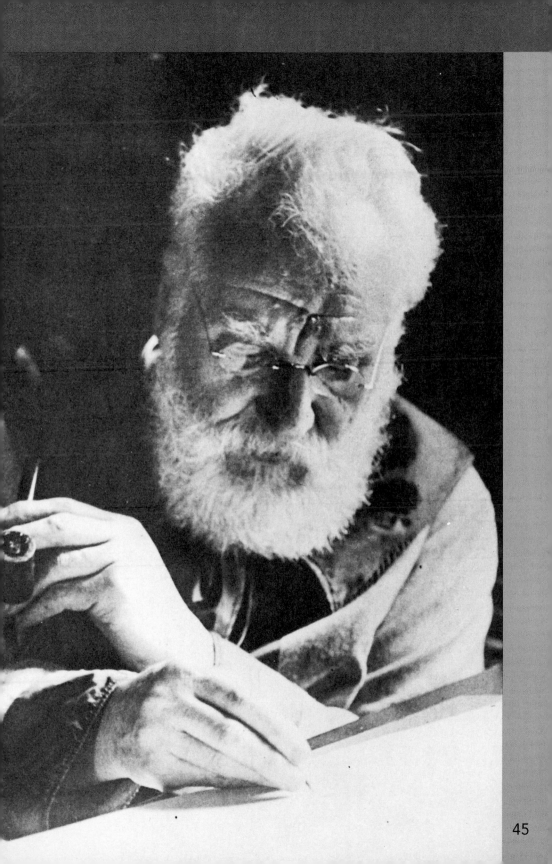

Bell Time Line

1847	Alexander Bell born in Edinburgh, Scotland, on March 3
1858	Adds Graham as his middle name
1862	Moves to London to study with his grandfather for one year
1863–1870	Goes to college in London and Edinburgh; teaches speech at various schools
1870	The entire Bell family moves to Brantford, Ontario, Canada
1871–1873	Moves to Boston; teaches speech at various schools and Boston University
1874	Starts doing experiments on speech and hearing; has idea for telephone
1875	Hires Thomas Watson as assistant; hears *ping*, which leads to telephone experiments
1876	Files patent application for telephone in February; first human speech heard on a telephone on March 10

1877		On July 9 starts Bell Telephone Company to offer people telephone service
1877	Marries Mabel Hubbard on July 11; has two children, Elsie May and Marian; two sons, Edward and Robert, die as infants	
1880	Invents the photophone	
1881	Improves Edison's phonograph and invents device to locate metal in a body	
1882	Becomes U.S. citizen	
1885	Forms AT&T (American Telephone & Telegraph Company) to handle long-distance calls for Bell Telephone and to make and sell telephones	
1887	Meets blind and deaf Helen Keller, age six, and helps family find a teacher	
1895–1909	Does experiments on flight and flying	
1915	Opens a telephone line between New York and San Francisco	
1922	Alexander Graham Bell dies in Nova Scotia, Canada, on August 2	

Index

Photo Credits: Oscar White/Corbis: 4; The Library of Congress: 6, 7, 8, 9, 14, 15, 18, 19, 23 (left), 27, 28-29, 36, 38, 45; Bettmann/Corbis: 12, 29; Bell Canada Historical Collection: 16; Corbis: 23 (right); United States Patent and Trademark Office: 26; SPL/Photo Researchers, Inc.: 31; Alexander Graham Bell National Historic Site of Canada: 39; The Granger Collection: 40-41; David Lawrence/Corbis: 42.

Library of Congress cataloging-in-publication data available.

ISBN 13: 978-0-439-83381-3   ISBN 10: 0-439-83381-7

10 9 8 7 6 5 4 3 2   07 08 09 10

Printed in the U.S.A. 23 • First printing, September 2007
Book design by Nancy Sabato